# 23

POEMS BY *Harshini Reddy*

ISBN 978-81-8465-097-6
Published by Harshini Reddy Parvatha
7-1-214/12, Ameerpet, Hyderabad, A.P., 500 016.
India. harshini.23book@gmail.com
www.harshinireddy.com

Book design: J Menon, www.grantha.com

Distributed by

 An initiative by the Outlook Group
retail@outlookindia.com
Ph: +91 80 25585275

The proceeds of this book will go to:
Support Cancer Awareness Foundation
www.supportcancerawareness.com

*I dedicate this book to ...*
Tejo Ananth Reddy
Aditi Reddy
Pranav Ponnaluri
Keshav Reddy
Milan Rao

## twenty three

She was young, independent and smart.

She lived in her own fantasy

and she had a perfect life

The only thing that could make

it more perfect was....

To find the "perfect guy"!

# Contents

# The Dreamer

She dreamed of a perfect life
Flying up to higher skies
She was the laughter in the breeze

She was the light in the sun's feast
She was the star in the midnight's crease
All she had to do was find the perfect guy

Who would never make her cry
And take her up to touch the sky
She lived in a fantasy

A place for no reality
She wished on a wishing star
Praying for no calamity

She had the love and the jealousy
She had her friends and her deities
All she needed was some reality

She waited for a perfect life
She prayed for all the luck
She searched mighty high and low
But nowhere was her desire

Though, she had it all
She wanted something more
More than the daily flow

She dreamed of a perfect life
Flying up to higher skies

# Konichiwa

She walks with pride
With her comes grace and beauty
She is the tune in my song
She is the right in the wrong
She has a beautiful soul

And a heart of gold
She lifts my spirits
And keeps me going
When nothing else can even come close
She gives me strength to face everyday

A hope renewed to celebrate
From friends to best friends
From crushes to heart breaks
From fights to sleepovers
We've been through the good

We've been through the bad
We've been through it all
I've had my fair share of ups and downs
But nothing can pull me down

As she gives me faith to pass each day
With memories that make me smile
That can last a lifetime
She is my laughter

She is my tear
She is the fighter of all my fears
After all, she knows me best
She is my family
She is my sister
She is my best friend who never lets me
    lose hope!

# Dance Along…

Won't you dance with me?
Won't you take me away?
Feel the rhythm
Feel the beat
That lifts us off our feet
As we dance along…
Embrace the joy
Embrace the love
Embrace "us"
As we dance along …

To the music
To the happiness
And to the love that we share
Won't you dance with me?

Take me away…
Someplace far away
Where we can dance all night

We can dance all day
We can dance under the breaking dawn
We can dance under the starry night

Turn me around
And follow my lead
As we dance along....

To the night we longed
To the sweet memories
To the trust that never breaks
To the happiness and faith

Won't you dance with me?
Won't you take me away?
Someplace faraway...

# Eyes of a Stranger

I looked at you
And you looked away
Walking past,
You took my breath away.

I needed to see
What we could be
To communicate
And reach out to you

A simple glance
A broken conversation
That is all it took
To take my breath away

Through the eyes of a stranger
I saw today…
I laughed
I cried

I sighed
At this insanity
Oh god!
You take my breath away

# Always and Forever

Awkward glances
Secret smiles
Moonlit dreams
And injured hearts

I watch you watching me
I see you wanting me
I just know that we're meant to be

Reach out
Take my hand
The distance seems so prolonged
All I want is to heal

Find me and…
Be my "always"
Be my "forever"
It is time for a new beginning

Time for change
Time for laughter
Time to be just a kid

Have faith
And give "us" a chance
'Cause all we have is here
And all we have is now
So let's embrace it together!

## Together Forever

We were driving down the avenue
Talking about our lives
Drinking coffee in the midst of the cold night
Waiting for the sun to shine bright
Hoping that we could carry on forever
Through the pain and change
Everything seemed so right
But now as it's getting colder
And we are going a little further

Every night I miss you
I believe in the stars
And knowing that as long as they shine
We will be together till forever
But I can't be any stronger
Thought we could last longer
But all the times just seem to be fading away

Our love is dying away
All I want to do is reach out
And make it all last forever
Just like we said
We will be together till the stars shine
Till this world stops revolving
Till the day we die
Till the sun illuminates

We will be together
However cold it gets
We will be together till forever....

# Mind Reader

Empty conversations and distant
   confrontations
All the times we spent
All the nights we dreamt
I thought
You were the fire
You were the desire
But never a liar…

The perfect guy
Who would never make me cry
And take me to touch the sky

You misunderstood
All that you could
I'm not a mind reader
Not at all
Nothing less
Nothing more

How could I ever have known?
That you were torn
I'm not a mind reader
I can't tell
Don't know when we fell
'Cause I'm not a mind reader
Never was
Never will be

I'm just me
Plain old me
I'm not a mind reader
So forget all your pleads
'Cause you've got to scream
For me to see!

# A Miracle

Underneath the deep blue sky I could see
  your eyes
While we walked the street as we waited for
  a miracle
Our hands stretched out to cover the
  distance
But nothing seemed very right

The faded memories slowly dying away
The cherished promises disappearing
You were the one
You were my life
Why did you have to go and ruin it all?

You were the sky
You were my dreams
Then why did you have to let it go?

Looking back on everything that's been
Thinking of all the times we spent
Just makes me want to scream and shout

You were the sun
You were the moon
What happened to it all?
What broke us apart?
Who spoke for us?

You told me to let it just pass away
But …what can a girl do?
What can I say when there's no more time?

What didn't I do right?
Which part didn't you get?

Just… take it all away
Just heal me all over again..
With hands outstretched
As we await a miracle…

# The Morning Dream

As we walked along the empty street
You took my hand
Even though we were not meant to be
Never letting go
You spoke with your eyes that held me close
You touched my cheek
Promising to never let go

You said you'd show it all
The shimmer of the moon
The joy of the sun
The last drop of rain that would never fall
As the dawn broke above us
Refusing to let go, I closed my eyes

Hoping this moment…
Which was too perfect
Which was too real

Which was not life
Would last forever

We walked the street holding hands
Communicating with our eyes
As the leaves swayed
As the birds shrieked
As the tears brimmed within my own eyes
Finally letting go… we parted ways

# Incomplete Full-moon Night

Waiting for you to realize how much we are
    meant to be
I just wish you could see
The meaning of how I feel

No judgment in your eyes
Nothing that defies
So why won't you give us a try?
And make yourself mine

It has been so long
Since we sang our song
Through all this distant fog
Between these tinted wistful sobs
I wish I could make you mine

At the end of this incomplete full-moon night
I am waiting for the hopeful light
To show you why we need to fight

Because what we had was right
Even though it is taking almost all of my might
To move through this tide

So open your eyes and see all that is right
Why won't you take my hand?
And take me off this land
Where no one is in sight

I believe in fairy lights and twinkling stars
But nothing seems to heal these scars
You reached out and touched my cheek
Healing the pain which made me weak

As the days flashed by
Reflecting the dreams in your deep brown eyes
All the memories seemed to be mine
Through my faded mind
As I softly thought to myself
"It's been so long since we last sang our song."

# Fairy Lights

Closing my eyes in reminiscence
I watched the fairy lights in the distance
The final words with which you parted
An end before it started

When I looked in the distance
For the man I finally found
Nowhere were you around

The first time you asked me to dance
Was just by a lucky chance
As you were standing in doubt
I held my hand out

I glowed with a light
In the starry night
As I put up a fight
Not to fall in love at first sight

You sang along
To the upbeat song
And you held me strong
All night-long

Underneath that deep blue sky
I swore I could have flown
But I remember that night, as all I did was cry
Because who would have known that you
    would have lied?

# My Imperfect World

The snow globe with a perfect castle
Came crashing down today

Nobody reaches out
Nobody communicates
It was all over
It was never enough
Broken down in pain

Reaching for the answers
But failed in vain
How did I get here?
Thought you would be here to show me
   the way
But now I am here
And you are there

Miles separate us
Time doesn't make sense
All I can see is black and white
Nothing seems like it was
Is life always this hard?

Without you here
The strength to fight is gone
The hope for tomorrow is lost
The pride in me is fading
And my life seems to be slowly disappearing

The snow globe with a perfect castle
Came crashing down today

## My Strength

Every day passes by in a blur
Nothing to look forward to
Nothing to say
I want it all to become better
But everything remains the same

Life moves on
Whether you want it to or not
Sometimes people are forgotten
Sometimes people are cherished forever
I just wanted to say
That you are one of those people who help
    me face everyday

I know I always have you to look back to
And you know you have me
I couldn't ask for a better brother
I have the worst day ever and then I
    remember you

I hear your voice over the phone
And everything gets better
So I just wanted to say thank you for all the
times you were there

Wherever I go, you will always remain in
    my heart
All the memories we shared are still in
    my head
You will never be forgotten
'Cause that's the kind of brother you are
The kind I will always love
The kind I will never forget

# Queen of Hearts

She walked like a queen in the open night
She spoke like she owned the world
She loved like she couldn't care less
She was his light
She was his pride

Until the night came...
Broken down in pain,
Reaching out to reconnect
She was...
The apple of his eye
The day during his night
The stars in the sky
The love in his heart

Until the night came...
Losing all she had
She was...

The light from the morning sun
The melody in his soul
The song in his heart

Until the night came...
Crumbling into agony
Now, she knows that...
Loving was a tragedy
A fairy tale with a broken ending
Promises that kept on pending

She walked like a queen in the open night
She spoke like she owned the world
She loved like she couldn't care less

## So Far Away

As we zoomed along
Feeling the breeze
Letting the raindrops touch my cheek
You were next to me
Looking beyond for something new

New from the pain and jealousy
That has driven you through
The reflection of this world in your eyes
The embracing breeze at midnight
Waited for you to break…

But you reached out and glanced at the
    night sky
Hoping for an answer from the shining
    moon
Hoping for an answer in the starry night
    I wonder…

How did we get so far?
How did we fall so bad?
How did we let it go?

I guess it was never meant to be
But the piercing pain in your eyes
Made me see,
Made me want to take it all away and
   walk away
Made me want to hold your hand and
   tell you
"Everything's going to be okay"

The sky turned pink and yellow
But we still sat in the darkness waiting for a
   shooting star
The broken conversation and polite smile
Made me want to scream…
Made me want to reach out and make it all
   better

But all you did was look ahead
Never letting anything take you down
But what is the point
With all the shattered dreams and hopes

When there is nothing left to take
Nothing left to say
Nothing for us to do
And nothing more to love!

# You and Me

Love is…
The teardrops on a white rose
The scars on a healing heart
The happiness in my eyes
The song that I dance to
The message on my hand
The pain of a broken fantasy
The end of a new start
The day that we part
The light in the dark
The melody in my soul
Love is…
You and me

# Beneath Deep Green Eyes

As I looked at her
I saw a story
Beneath her deep green eyes
I saw a story

A tale of pain as well as tragedy
A fairy tale filled with broken fantasies
Her quivering lips spoke of fear
Her restless eyes searched near
For a miracle

A miracle that would erase the past
A miracle that would heal her soul

The broken promises let her see the world
  around her
The scarred heart revealed the lies and deceit
The harsh words echoed in her pretty head

A thousand tears and 2 years later
As I looked at her
The story was dying underneath her broken eyes
And the tale of misery was slipping away
The girl she was... slowly fading away...
Beneath her deep green eyes
I saw a story....

# What Do You Do...?

What do you do?
When nothing seems right
And everything is broken
When all you have is nothing
And all you know is crumbling

What do you do?
When numbness is frightening
And love is so dreading
When the resistance is fading
And all you have to do is keep on fighting

What do you do?
When the stars don't shine
And the sun doesn't give hope
When there is nothing left
Except the guilt and pain
That somehow keeps you going

What do you do?
When the love is binding
And the faith is ceasing
When the fire is freezing
And you are screaming

What do you do?
When you are bleeding
And there is nothing to do except pleading
When all you believe in
Has come crashing down

What do you do?
When you are screaming
And nothing is as seeming
When nobody is there to rescue you
And nobody is there to believe in
What do you do?

# Reflection of a Hidden Innocence

The innocent eyes stared back
With no sense of regret
With no sense of hope
For a new beginning
Her whole life awaited her
To enlighten those pretty brown eyes

A growing story
A budding dream that she will find soon
A fight for survival
All hidden deep underneath those mystic eyes

No endurance
No ways to please
Stared back towards the past
Looking in a wistful manner
At what could have been

Neither the tremor will be forgotten
Nor repeated in the past of her childhood
A red rose will never hold the same meaning
A teddy bear just won't have brown eyes
Christmas will dither to show the colors of
    green and red
Numbers will never mean the same
And love will never live up to its name

# Someday

Someday I will find all the answers
Until then I will just hold on
Hold on to all our dreams
All the times we spent talking about our lives
Looking for the right choice

Someday I'm going to fly high
Reach out and touch the sky
Someday I will find all the answers
Waiting for the future
To take me
Somewhere faraway

Where love is the only answer
And faith is the only prayer
On this magical night
All I want to do is find meaning
Somewhere in these shining stars

All I need is to find my place
Somewhere in this universe
All I have is a drop of hope
Somewhere deep within me

Cause I know that
Someday I will find my love
Someday I will find myself
Someday I will find all the answers

# Life is "Now"

Life is here
Life is now
Life is only you and I

The past may be gone forever
And the future doesn't know what it holds
But this is your life
Right here
Right now

Take all the chances
Take all the love as well as the pain
Look for tomorrow
Learn from the past
You never know how long life can last

Show them what you are
And never give up
Keep the faith as well as the hope

Fight for belief
Fight till you win
Fight for yourself and keep holding on
No matter what

I am looking over you
Looking to take away the hurt and misery
from you
This is your life
This is your chance
To prove this unreal world all wrong

Give it your best shot
And never look back
Because life is here
Life is now
It's never someplace else.

# Purple Shaded Memories

Holding back on the memories
As the tears fill my shaded eyes
All I can see is the distant times
And all that rhymes

You were the one who showed me the way
Took my hand and promised to stay
Stay by my side
Till the end of this tide

Don't let me fall
For you are the sun in my broken heart
You are the moon when all is dark
For you are the one who makes my eyes spark

As the purple shades fill my empty soul
You reached out when I was cold
As the footprints sinned my mind
You let me free when nothing was mine

As the sun set low
You never let go
You taught me the way
And all there is to show

Now, I want you to know
Sometimes you are pushed around
And all you can do is hope
Hope for the light that is not at sight

Even though nothing is as it seems
Never give up on your dreams
Hold them tight
And never let them go without a fight

I love you my friend
More than you know
I love you my friend
More than I show

## Inspiration, Motivation and My Fixation!

Woke up in the morning light
Didn't think you would leave my side
Last night it was all so right
Then why did we fight?

You were my inspiration
My motivation
The fixation that got me through

Now I'm looking for something new
I know it's out there
Waiting to be found soon
But just can't see it through
Through all this morning dew
Whatever am I supposed to do?

It haunts me fast
I am stuck in the past

I need some inspiration
I need a new fixation
That gets me through these lonely nights
And all the times we had those fights

Nothing seems so real
Nobody feels my soul
Nowhere to go
Nobody to know

Didn't need the pain
Feels so insane
Need to go places
But this is what came
Need the love to get me through

Need the inspiration
Motivation
My fixation

# Fight

Fight for the hope that got you through
Fight for the love that you never knew
Fight for this world's lost dreams
Fight for the night you screamed

Never let go
Never give up
This is your time to shine
And show the world what you've got

Fight for the answers deep within
Fight for the faith that brought you here
Fight for the people in your world

You have one life
You have one goal
You have one chance to show
Show the world what you've got

Whether it is a dream come true
Or a fantasy renewed
Fight for yourself
Fight with all you've got
Fight against the pain that was cruel

Take the risk and win it all
Show the world what you've got
This is your last chance
This is your only life
This is your last breath
To show the world what you've got

# The Beginning

Life takes you many ways
You never know where you may end up
At the end, all we have is what we fought for
All we know is what we have learnt

There is nothing more wondrous than our
    creation
But sometimes I wonder…
Even after the pain, tears and heartache
What makes us go on…?

When the tears don't end and the pain
    doesn't stop
What more can we do…?
When everything is done and over!

Just hope for the light that follows the
    thunder
Just wish for the day that follows the night

Pray for courage and have faith within
   yourself

Because one day it will all be over
And then the time and pain taken to get
   there
Won't matter anymore!

# An Ode to Happiness!!!

A hundred miles I walked to get to you
A broken heart and endless teardrops

To reach you, it seemed to take a lifetime
Half kept promises and unforgiving words
   made me lose all hope
But who would have known that I'd finally
   meet you?

The circle of life took me places
Too many for my age
High expectations and rash decisions
Left me empty from within
But who would have thought you would
   take it all away?

Fighting back for strength
Pushing myself through
Seemed hard enough

But who would have guessed that it would
　all seem so easy now?

Humble requests and faltered choices
I thought I would never reach you
Who would have seen us meeting
　someday?

For you, I will put up a constant fight
After all, "Happiness" is the only way

# One in A Million

A magical night it was
The air filled with mystery
When the curtain was drawn

Her bright eyes shining in the light
Her lips curved into a perfect smile
Her long black hair in her face
She glanced from side to side

One in a million
Who stands out of the crowd
Watching in silence
She stands out

The way she walks
The way she talks
This is her world
This is her ramp to shine

Lifting her head
She leads the crowd
The money, the fame and name
She's all what she wanted
And more than that

She's the dream of the haunted past
She's the aura of the present
She's the queen of the near future

She's the beginning
She's the ending
She's one in a million
Grace and beauty and all

# Twenty Three

Then she realizes what
Everybody else knew all along...

You cannot live in your own bubble
And sometimes you are pushed out of it
Which may cause heartache and pain
But at the end, you should lift up
Your magic wand
And conjure up your potion for survival...
Then... you will be "one in a million."

*My sincere thanks to my parents
who are always there for me and
support me all along.
It is only because of them that
this book was possible.*

*I love you*